PRAISE for *Sighs and*

Poetry is a gift that is meant to be shared. Poets see things differently. They observe, study the situation, and then put their thoughts and ideas into word pictures to share with others.

In this collection of poems, the poet takes the reader on a journey from "Alarum" to "Los Desaparecidos" to "Walpurgisnacht." You will marvel at the superb artistry of his words. The reader is invited to take a word journey as the poet reviews past experiences, his joy of life, and his dreams of future endeavors—allowing the poet and the reader to blend into the unity of thought.

Geza's poetry stirs the soul, challenges the mind, and comforts the heart. Be prepared for a very good read.

Joan M. Lacombe, Poet Laureate Aiken, SC

Geza Tatrallyay's poetry is a feast for the ear and the imagination. These are poems to be both read and heard to be fully appreciated.

Rebecca McMeekin,
Organizer of Randolph PoemTown

Geza Tatrallyay's artfully crafted poems invoke the existential dilemmas of a life long-lived, in which relationships among mind, body, and soul are constantly reexamined and juxtaposed. His poems teem with a delighted playfulness around word-sounds ("a mere/mirrored/mirage of untold lies") and invented words that animate the poet's scrutiny of everything from a squashed crab to mental and physical deterioration.

Deming P. Holleran,
Poet Laureate Hanover, NH

SIGHS AND MURMURS

GEZA TATRALLYAY

PUBLISHING

P.R.A. Publishing
P.O. Box 211701 Martinez, GA 30917
www.prapublishing.com

ISBN 978-1941416-12-9 paperback
ISBN 978-1941416-13-6 e-book

Library of Congress Control Number: 2017951970

The poem *Café Scene* was published in *SunStruck Magazine*, Vol. 2, no. 2,
April 2016.

For Orlando

ACKNOWLEDGMENTS

I would like to thank Lucinda Clark for undertaking the publishing of this, my second collection of poems, and for arranging numerous readings that have allowed me to bring these and the poems in *Cello's Tears*, my other volume, to a broader public.

TABLE OF CONTENTS

INTRODUCTION

███

Sighs and Murmurs is the second collection of poems that I have written over many years and in many different cultural contexts. The first, *Cello's Tears*, published in May 2015 by P.R.A. Publishing and receiving strong critical acclaim, similarly brought together poems composed during my life in many countries, with several influenced by works in other artistic media or other languages.

In *Sighs and Murmurs,* too, I have included such works, notably one that was inspired by the 1972 film by Ingmar Bergman, about which the director himself observed that he had "touched wordless secrets that only the cinema can discover."[1] (The title is an allusion to the film, as well.) In Part II of this volume, titled *Mo(u)rning* (after the first poem), I challenge this contention and explore the ability of poems to communicate the innermost self, however inadequately.

The second poem inspired by another medium, *"Fencer Relaxing,"* was influenced by a wonderful pen-and-ink drawing by my good friend Jeremy Smith, the Canadian painter of the High Realist School, who used me as a model for this work. This appears in Part I of the volume, titled *Fluidbeing* (again, the title of one of the poems in the section), which explores the search for definition and meaning in human existence.

Part III of the collection, titled *Rubble*, delves into the destructive side of man. The first poem, "Café Scene," takes a poem I originally wrote in 1973 in Paris and adds to it a second section written on a visit soon after some of the recent terrorist events that have lamentably changed the City of Light forever. The ultimate poem in this section and the collection, *"The Last Quake,"*

---

[1] Jerry Vermilye (1 January 2002). *Ingmar Bergman: His Life and Films*. McFarland, p. 123.

1

touches—with a very light brush—on the destructive power of nature, of which man is only a small part.

Several of the works included here experiment with language (e.g., "Fluidbeing," "For a Squashed Land Crab," "A Lover's Introspection," "Mo(u)-rning"), and/or form (most obviously, "Dream, choreographed" and "Act of Resignation"), while others are more traditional in shape and poetic usage. In fact, some make reference to classical Western and Eastern literature and thought.

As with *Cello's Tears*, I thoroughly enjoyed writing and compiling this collection, and sincerely hope that the reader will find similar pleasure in perusing the poems in this little volume.

Geza Tatrallyay
Barnard, VT

I. FLUIDBEING

FLUIDBEING

The mind grows from the seed,
feeding on all around—
a balloon that expands
with each mouthful of air.

One more inhalation,
and it bursts; it explodes
into infinity,
deflates, destroying all.

Being becomes fluid,
recedes to its point source,
the dimensionless void
where good and bad are one.

And there remains only
a lifeless plastic skin
without definition:
a skin we try to stretch
over frantic knuckles
to reestablish form,
to find meaning somewhere,
a modus vivendi.

But there is no power
in the lung any more,
no desire drives the need:
skin molts from dead knuckles,
blubber melts to a stench,
vultures of emptiness
strip off remaining flesh,
gouge out eyes, cheek and tongue,
and peck at the brain cells,
relishing destruction;
all, all is gobbled up
to the last marrow cell.

And the mind substance floats
in total abstraction,
no longer tenable
by earthly dimensions.

FOR A SQUASHED LAND CRAB

In the twilight trauma
of the beach at Ixtapa
a land crab sallied forth
from its dungeon in the sand:

he caught my eye in his,
he fathomed me—
and I think I him:

I willed him life,
life to life,
and he it
back to me—

but in that marvelous moment
of trans-special spiritflow,
a hulking stud
should trod upon
my comrade crab:

so now the crab is only was,
and my spirit, my eyes, lie limp
bleeding in the sandpapersand.

FENCER, RELAXING
(*Hommage à Jeremy Smith**)

Myself, there, on the wall,
staring knowingly,
blankly, into the void:

a relaxed,
architectural slouch
(or is it the
tortured crouch
of defeat and
humiliation?)

a lifelike rendition
in blacks and whites and grays:
(is my face, though,
not too pallid?)

Limbs, like girders,
creating space,
akin to a Moore;

muscles tightened,
tendons tensing
across jutting bones,

folds of skin over flesh,
and oh,
that fatigued,
ancient face of cognition . . .

---

* *A good friend, Jeremy Smith, a top Canadian realist artist, did a pen-and-ink picture titled "Fencer, Relaxing" for which he used me as the model. That work inspired this poem.*

8

on the right,
a scaly,
reptilian towel,
slithering to life,
like a nascent larva
(soon to be me)
emerging from some
non-existent cocoon . . .

by the wall,
an unfinished row
of spectating,
metallic chairs,
ignoring
the unfolding
human drama—
a white towel
draped over one,
shroud-like,
waiting . . .

on the left,
a soiled
and sinister
fencing jacket
(the cocoon discarded—
or is it the empty soul
outward bound?)
hanging, like
Michelangelo's skin,
invading
the regimented
order of the wall . . .

down below,
a faceless mask
(even more deathly
than my ashen face)
severed from the body,
resting unnaturally
on a fencing bag,
pregnant,
like a polished coffin
with the dismembered remains . . .

by the mask,
epées are crossed,
arm-like,
nonchalantly,
resigned in defeat . . .

and everywhere,
those wires,
those worm-like,
senseless wires
boring under the skin,
into the brain,
and the very soul
of the universe . . .

and there,
in between
the hanging skin
and the faceless mask,
that horrific machine
with those bulging,
blinking,
insect eyes
(could this be the soul,
naked and smiling
in its journey
out of earthly life?)

in this progress
of time through space,
of birth toward death,
among all these
different textures
of bounded life
and infinite
nothingness,
only the human
I am complete
in my defiance
of the unknown,
empty universe.

COLD MORNING

A gray day dawns
portending snow

The radio
says a blizzard

Cold penetrates
beneath the sheets

I cannot raise
myself from bed

I just lie there and
compose this poem

SHORT OF MADNESS

Fleeting atoms of existence
flirt
with an all too serious mind,

that strains to contain
life
in a plastic sheath of understanding:

what balloon
will not burst
in madness
when it embraces this *Walpurgisnacht*?

TORPOR OF MIDDLINGNESS

the torpor of middlingness pervades the being,
settles on the self and crushes activity:

ambition tires with old age:
we become dried out husks of life—
no more the fertile loves of youth—
gone the child-eye view of the world—
our great expectations have shrunk
to an empty kernel of truth:

the endless nothingness of death.

HERMES

the path is alive
under scrambling feet
with passion from earth

its tail whips behind
propelling forward
faster and faster

bird calls merge with forest green
pine pricks with musty odors
drops of sweat with boiling skin

everything all around
convulses in a frenzy
of frantic vibration
and melts into some liquid

and I
eternal runner
having reduced the world
soar with ecstasy
found in a moment
that has enslaved all

Truth
      Beauty
            Freedom
Happiness
      and Love
and all that rot.

REFLECTIONS OF A REFLECTION

I

A youth
in a boat
on a motionless sea

madly stones
a reflected
alter ego
whose serene
water apparition
would stare
glassy-eyed
forever
into an empty
and infinite sky

perfect ripple circles
lash the waxen dead figure
into primordial frenzy
jolting it spasmodically
to a Pinocchio life

II

Only
when the fatal wind
begins to blow

does the idle spirit wake

Pinocchio panics

and

as if possessed

moves across the waters
in a wild demonic dance

III

Too late
too late
this eruption of life

condemning clouds
of age and anonymity
strangle the aimless puppet

and everything disappears
forgotten in the fog

WE WALK YOU AND I . . .

We walk
you and I
under the trees
dripping from the morning rain
in the grass
frozen the night before
and now covered
with the falling hopes of autumn.

We walk
you and I
but where are we going?

The rays of the fading sun
lead us toward the waterfall
as if it were spring again
and we could cool our panting bodies
not in the salty tears of a love remembered
but in the spring of eternity.

We walk
you and I
but where are we going?

PASSING

A goddess
on a park bench
screamed
with her eyes
at passing me,

screamed
a pitiful plea
from solitary eyes,

screamed at me passing
among pecking pigeons
wading
through the dung of pampered dogs,
those paper hulls
and beer can carcasses.

Only in the wild
purified space
of an invisible mind
did I dare
lunge toward her
and kiss
and love her
with all my might.

And when I turned
to delight
in one more glimpse

an empty bench
screamed at me
from among all the dung and corpses.

PARADE

In the Jardin de Luxembourg
    I sit and wait.

Grateful
    that the cold winter sun
    destroys my thoughts
sucks me with its web of rays
from the spectacle of reality
cavorting before my eyes.

I do not see the small children
playing with their sailboats and cars,
nor the *vieillards* shuffling cards
in their tattered old coats and hats;

I do not see the bourgeois walking,
en famille, the Sunday afternoon,
nor the lovers playing at love,
all enwebbed in each other.

I feel only the wind
strike my face
with the tears
of the fountain
that has watched
for centuries.

HAIKU: TEPID IS THE TEA

tepid is the tea
in the cup I once gave you:
our love too is cold

ROMANTIC HYPERBOLE

the moon's
slender
sliver slams
in my face:

I love you,
and you are
as far away . . .

FOOTPRINTS IN THE SAND

I walk upon a lonely beach
a storm gathering out at sea.

I walk
I walk to no purpose
with thoughts
lost among grains of sand.

Wind and darkness
walk with me in my solitude
holding my hands
leading me on.

There are no footprints here
except those of the wind
and the darkness.

Waves beat against my mind
and grains of sand
roll down my cheeks
to disappear in the void
that surrounds me.

I search for light
a star
a fire.

I await the storm eagerly
hoping its fury will wipe all away
and everything will be renewed again.

A LOVER'S INTROSPECTION

fleshmeldedwithflesh
in
purported
love

vanity   ecstasy

CHRISTMAS AND AFTERTHOUGHTS

Christmas, and crystal snow flecks drop
from an invisible heaven,
(like grains of sand in an hourglass),
vanishing, ghoul-like, on contact
with a cemented over earth:
their descent through the empty night,
too fast and short-lived: (what sorrow,
what pain, when a child dies!) no time,
there is no time for their beauty—
their timeless, infinite beauty—
to blossom and inflame our love.

Only the flakes know their perfection.

II. MO(U)RNING

MO(U)RNING

The morning of the years
has come
and gone.

Like a beloved friend
who passed away
we remember
morning.

Like a dream
we strain to remember
the morning
but cannot.

I cry
for that unrealized ideal
that was
but is no longer real
is no longer real.

I cry
for the morning.

There is only
the night.

CRIES AND WHISPERS
(After Bergman)

Odious fragments
of childhood terror
of nighttime panic
clamor for entry
to the lonely mind:

    cries and whispers
    without substance
    surface
    from the depths of being

    cries and whispers
    half-heard
    tear the silence
    of a soul's solitude

    sighs of an ungraspable realm
    reverberate
    within the prison of the mind
    jamming reason

    and escape amplified
    in a piercing screech of panic
    a timeless infinite horror
    transcending human imagination
    invades the soul from beyond death
    and annihilates the bounds of mortality

The being cannot cope.

The being self-destructs.

DREAM, CHOREOGRAPHED

Background: Bleak
hillock,
leafless trees,
obscure sky:

Foreground: my
black back,
and I
gazing
in terror
toward
the stark mound:

And in between: a white steed,
translucent,
yes, ghost-like,
gallops among dead trees
toward the horizon.

Aftermath: I wake,
the dream
vanishes,
and then
even
its memory dies.

ACT OF RESIGNATION

1.   gangrenous flows
       fornicate in
       a stack of stars

2a.   Socrates' soul
       dances naked
       with vapor gods

  b.   light years above
       canals of danglingling
       corpses

  c.   that breathe wails of release
       and count the our fathers
       the crucifix still owes

3.   hemlock shapes approach in the receding
       footsteps of a futile faustian pact

4.   my friends my ideas
       my stamp collection
       whimper in a hell
       teeming with a crazed
       slobbering mankind
       and all of godkind

5a.   and I too
       seem to have
       said goodbye
       to my soul

  b.   left it chained
       to a star
       danglingling
       rotrotting

6.   amen.

MORNING THOUGHTS

All around
neural impulses
incorporate,
one more time,
out of the night's
oblivion:

light seeps through
the gray mist,
shakily heralds
another fetal day
emerging from the
wrinkled womb of the world . . .

alas: the morn's
passing freshness,
its pregnant
ions of ozone
soon evanesce:

the day's
obvious
drudgery
usurps
the globe
from east
to west . . .

the outstanding hope:
that tomorrow's morning
will be eternal.

STUDIES IN DISLOCATION

I

A bullfrog ribbits
from the lily pond
waking my senses
from inside silence
to outside thunder.

II

A ghost train whistles
an ominous screech
and derails my brain
from its peaceful track.

III

A telephone rings
and rings in my dream
till I jolt upright:
I rub sleepy eyes
saunter to the phone
and forget the dream.

But the phone is dead.

WHEN I CONSIDER . . .

When I consider
these measly morsels
of joy and sorrow
thrown to us mortals
in playful disdain,

When I consider
how much men cherish
such feeble feelings,
how they pray and wish
for love and friendship,

And when I regard
the eternity
of unfeeling time,
the infinity
of unloving space,

Pathos crushes me
And I weep in pain.

SHADOWS

A foggy veneer
filters the world beyond:
through this opaque pane
I see distorted shapes
seeming to beckon,
as if almost human—

fairy silhouettes
step a demonic dance
in the grey nothing
outside my consciousness—

but I ask myself:
are they really beyond
the translucent glass,
or are they just shadows
on that outer skin,
that nebulous limit—

shadows of my mind,
those darkest dreams and thoughts
that yearn to break out,
to transcend my humanity?

NOSTALGIA (NOTWITHSTANDING)

I

murmurs
of a faded memory
fidget somewhere inside

dreams
from withered ages
strum on frayed strings
boldly bridging
birth
and the ever budding now

a painful nostalgia
punctures
the skull's
sheltering cocoon

and the severed nerves
of childhood fancies
bleed once again

the flesh
weeps in eulogy
for that touch
from innocence
and a mere
mirrored
mirage
of untold lies

II

one fleeting glimpse
over the approaching rise
toward that frozen sunset
stagnating in eternity

exposes
to an age-worn traveler
the barren destination
of his residual mind

alone
in the evening's
bleeding glow
a frantic odysseus
wistfully turns
and merges
into the safe fog
of memories
behind

WHERE AM I . . .

Where am I
that the sun
does not rise
that there are
no flowers

Where am I
that the sky
is darkness
and the earth
charred ashes

Faces do not smile
and empty eye sockets stare
from rubbery masks on pedestals

Hollow stumps stand
in the rubble
of fallen monuments of stone

Carcasses are strewn
on concrete streets
and the silence echoes
the noise of the morgue

I can feel it
I can feel it

The void is in me
on me
all around me
devouring me
I am nothing
and there is
nothing.

A SHADOW CALLED MEMORY
(After a Poem in Spanish By X.S.)

it was a night
that ended
that same morning
with a desperate
palpitation:
paling
in the distance
I could see
the indigenous colors
of our heavenly home

time passed
and in my mind
I read
a memory
that will stay
all my life
a sweet dream
that cannot
be forgotten
upon waking

time paused:
its crazed
unchainable force
rang the bells
of a solitary end
within those colorful walls

slowly my arms
embraced
that memory
of enchantment
and pleasure

my seed
bursting
and bursting
in the warmth
of your abdomen

what intoxicating touch
what
what has clouded
our clear and pure fate?

perhaps we should blame
the fingers
of that ancient moon
the fingers
that so promptly
opened an abyss
between you and me.

EMBER EYES

Embers
glower
in the dark

like
your
eyes

that find me
when they seek
someone else

WINTRY WINDS

wintry winds steal
summer's glow

white sheets of snow
shroud earth's smile

while I only die

FIRN

an arctic chill
churns
across the firn,

like in my heart
when death
blows near.

Firn is defined as granular snow, especially on the upper part of a glacier, where it has not yet been compressed into ice.

III. RUBBLE

CAFÉ SCENE

I
(Paris, 1973)

I have put my guts
on the shelf,
and I dance
alone
all the tangos of Paris.

In the cafés
I talk to myself,
discussing inflation
and Picasso's death.

Facing the mirror,
I see them laugh
and gesticulate,
nod and jabber
on and on
about this and that.

And nauseated by the smoke,
the noisy mob,
I read my Dostoevsky,
snubbing at life.

II
(Paris, 2015)

I take my guts down
from the shelf
and I tread
alone
all the streets of Paris.

In the cafés
I talk to myself,
discussing the horror
at the Bataclan.

Facing the mirror,
I see them come
brandishing their
Kalashnikovs
randomly
firing at the crowd.

And nauseated by the blast,
the bloody scene,
I read my Charlie Hebdo,
snubbing at death.

LOS DESAPARECIDOS

Prostrate, a mother pleas for her disappeared son,

as if he were still flesh and blood, living tissue

(that cringes from the cattle prod, and trembles in
ashen anticipation of the trampling boot)

and not just broken bones scattered in some mass grave,
or a puffed-up, mangled corpse floating, throat slit
and anonymous, in the sewage of the Plate . . .

the silent procession of mourning mothers masks
the deluge of desperate tears that has sculpted
these aging faces—tears for those disappeared ones . . .

but you, Argentina,
you do not weep;
coward,
you dare not cry;
you are no
mother
to your sons.

NIGHTMARE

I had a dream last night,
A dream of a fair youth
Lying behind steel bars,
Crying in the darkness,
Bleeding, mutilated.

I wanted to reach him,
Help and comfort the boy,
Suffering behind bars,
Face contorted in pain:
But something held me back.

I yearned to touch his soul,
To ease his blinding pain,
To say a prayer for him,
Dying behind those bars:
But something held me back.

Then he cried out to me—
But I did not help him;

I just stood there and watched him die,
A blank expression on my face,
And then quietly walked away.

PATHÉTIQUE, OR FAMINE IN ETHIOPIA VIEWED ON ST. NICHOLAS' DAY

Millions of limbs
hang
limply
from bloated torsos,

Yolkless corneas
grope
blindly
from pock-scarred faces,

While we reach
limply
bearing token gifts,

While we stare
blindly
watching mankind die.

PRAYER

Passer-by:

do not kick,

rather kiss,
this cringing cur—

it may be you.

MONUMENT AND SKY

Stone soldier,
standing proudly:
an eternal silhouette
against a bleeding sky,

you stare
blindly
into the burning heavens
that hint
at an unfathomable inferno.

Down that tired,
dusty highway,
soldier of stone,
can you not see
tomorrow's blood
spill across the sky?

(Will you then,
soldier of stone,
lay down your gun
and shed a tear
with me for all
humankind?)

ALARUM

the plangent wail of a Siren shrieking
grates above the rubble of imminent
destruction:

        our imperfect ears refuse
to admit the Stentor's admonition

'though all around,
             rat and 'roach
                   flee
                    panic-
stricken,
      from this concrete Sodom,
                   this Hell:

while we,
      the cognoscenti,
           lovingly

unite, to raise a tower of Babel
(building Chaos with our bombs and missiles)
toward a heaven that we think we know

A SINGED, BARREN PLANET BROODS . . .

a singed, barren planet broods
below a burning heaven,
and smolders internally
with fear and hate and anger:

      bombs screaming,
      deafening
      booms and bursts
      of acrid
      explosives,
      unearthly
      shrieks of war's
      shocked victims,
      souls wrenching;

echoes heard above this tottering vista:

tears of widows and orphans,
of mothers of dead sons,
of lovers of soldiers
flow freely in catharsis:

will this weeping wash away war's
horrible annihilation
and restore the splendor of the world?

SCRATCH

We are
men
who drink
the blood of
men
who drink
the blood of
men
who drink
the blood of
men
who drink
the blood of
men
who drink
the blood of
men . . .

Can't we change the damned record?

THE LAST QUAKE

Earth opened its mouth today,
and almost died of laughter.
Mankind panicked. And perished:
victim of the mirth of earth.

ABOUT THE AUTHOR

Born in Budapest, Geza Tatrallyay escaped with his family from Hungary in 1956, during the Revolution and immigrated to Canada. He has represented Canada as a Rhodes Scholar, as a host in the Ontario Pavilion during Expo '70, the world's fair in Osaka, Japan, and as an Olympic fencer in the Montreal 1976 games. He is a graduate of Harvard and Oxford Universities, as well as the London School of Economics.

Tatrallyay is a prolific writer. He has published thrillers (*Arctic Meltdown, Twisted Reasons,* and *Twisted Traffick*), a memoir about his family's escape (*For the Children*), and a second one about his efforts to help three Czechoslovak hostesses at Expo '70 defect to Canada (*The Expo Affair*) as well as *Cello's Tears*, his first collection of poetry. He is currently completing work on several projects in the thriller genre as well as the last of the memoirs in the Cold War escape series. *Sighs and Murmurs* is his second book of poetry. Tatrallyay is a citizen of both Canada and Hungary. He and his wife, Marcia, now divide their time between San Francisco and Barnard, Vermont, with frequent trips back to the many places they have lived, including New York, Boston, Montreal, Toronto, London, Frankfurt, Budapest, Vienna, Bordeaux, and Montevideo. They have two children, Alexandra and Nicholas, and two grandsons, Sebastian and Orlando.